Indelible

Becky Gould Gibson

The Broadkill River Press
Milton, Delaware

Acknowledgments

"The Lydian Woman Speaks to the Dead Saint" ['There is neither Jew nor Greek. . .' Galatians 3:28] will appear in *Third- and Fourth-Wave Catholic Women Writers: The Future of Unruly Women in the Church,* the anthology's fourth volume, which will be published by SUNY Press in 2019. I wish to thank the editors of that publication.

Many thanks to friends and family who read the evolving draft of *Indelible* with generosity and discernment: Claire and John Lamiman, Janet Joyner, Carol and John Stoneburner, Charles Gibson, and Bill Gibson. To Kathleen Graber for her workshop on poetry manuscript at the Vermont College of Fine Arts Post-Graduate Writers' Conference; in particular, her perspective on voice helped me to achieve clarity in this book. And special thanks to Dr. Thomas J. Haupert for his meticulous translation of Acts16: 14-15 from Koine Greek into English.

Indelible (c) Becky Gould Gibson 2018
ISBN 978-1-940120-79-9
Library of Congress Control Number:
2018962438

cover photo
Philippi
(c)LeeAbbamonte.com

Published by the Broadkill River Press
Milton, Delaware

Indelible

To the memory of
Elizabeth Conlan Gregg
(1932-2018)

muse, mentor, friend

Acts 16:12-15—

And from thence to Philippi, which is the chief city of that part of Macedonia, and a colony: and we were in that city abiding certain days.

Though I am called Lydia   Lydia is not my name

And on the Sabbath we went out of the city by a river side, where prayer was wont to be made; and we sat down and spoke unto the women which resorted thither.

I am from that region
my master a purple merchant who taught me the trade
I got good at it   so good
my head for the business of bolts exceeded even his

And a certain woman named Lydia, a seller of purple, of the city of Thyatira, which worshipped God, heard us: whose heart the Lord opened, that she attended to the things spoken of Paul.

sebomene   devout woman
theosebes   God fearer God reverer
names I'd not choose for myself were I the one choosing

And when she was baptized, and her household, she besought us saying, If ye have judged me to be faithful to the Lord, come into my house . . . .

Now listen
listen after all those centuries thumbing past on thin pages
never stopping to ask me who I am
or waiting to hear my answer
Search all you want among these ruins

these endless ancient inscriptions
no scrap of purple   no loom or spindle
you'll find nothing of me   know nothing of me
unless I tell you you will never know   never even know my name

Table of Contents

The River Speaks to the Pilgrim	9
The Lydian Woman Speaks with the Pilgrim	11
Philippi to Thyatira, November, 49 CE	13
Thyatira to Philippi, Early March, 50 CE	15
Philippi to Thyatira, Late March, 50 CE	17
The Lydian Woman Speaks with *Christianity Today*	20
Thyatira to Philippi, August, 50 CE	22
The Lydian Woman Speaks with a Buyer from Milan	24
Via Egnatia: A Road-Stone Speaks to the Pilgrim	26
Philippi to Thyatira, Late October, 50 CE	28
The Lydian Woman Speaks with *The Christian Science Monitor*	30
Philippi to Corinth, Early February, 51 CE	32
The Lydian Woman Speaks with the Pilgrim	34
Corinth to Philippi, Late April, 51 CE	36
Philippi to Corinth, June, 51 CE	38
The Lydian Woman Speaks to the Dead Saint	40
Thyatira to Philippi, Early September, 51 CE	42
The Lydian Woman Speaks to the Dead Saint	44
Philippi to Thyatira, March, 52 CE	46
The Road-Stone Speaks to the Pilgrim	48
The Lydian Woman Speaks with *Ms. Magazine*	49
Philippi to Ephesus, April, 52 CE	51
The Lydian Woman Speaks with the Pilgrim	53
Thyatira to Philippi, Late October, 52 CE	55
Philippi to Ephesus, March, 53 CE	57
Ephesus to Philippi, Late April, 53 CE	59

The Lydian Woman Speaks to the Dead Saint	61
Philippi to Caesarea, Prison, December 57 CE	63
The Road-Stone Speaks to the Pilgrim	65
The Lydian Woman Speaks to the Dead Saint	66
Rome to Philippi, May, 60 CE	68
The Lydian Woman Speaks to the Dead Saint	70
Philippi to Rome, January, 61 CE	72
Rome to Philippi, April, 61 CE	74
The Lydian Woman Speaks to the Dead Saint	76
Rome to Philippi, August, 61 CE	78
The Lydian Woman Speaks to the Dead Saint	80
Rome to Philippi, May, 62 CE	82
The Lydian Woman Speaks with a Supplier from Cairo	84
The Lydian Woman Speaks to the Dead Saint	86
Philippi to Rome, Early April, 63 CE	88
Rome to Philippi, June, 63 CE	89
Ostia to Philippi, Late August, 64 CE	91
The Lydian Woman Speaks with the Pilgrim	93
The Road-Stone Speaks to the Pilgrim	95
The Lydian Woman Speaks to the Dead Saint	96
NOTES	98
About the Author	100

The River Speaks to the Pilgrim

                The Gangites outside the ruins at Philippi

She has not come this way for some time.
She may be dead.
On that morning, men I'd never seen were here
when she arrived.
Oh, I'd long known the woman.
She often bathed with others
before Dionysus.
Then as now a nice spot—
willows, fig trees, oaks—gods in all places.

One called Paulus took a word from his pocket,
a word I'd not heard, tossed the word
like a stone into my waters.
Christos.
The man was of small stature,
his voice too large for his body.
I did not trust it.
Christos.
The word would not sink for gravity's sake.
I felt nothing.

The man motioned her toward him.
She entered willingly, yet not quite yielding,
shuddered from my cold.
Christos.
Say it. Say you believe.
She hesitated.
Shifted her weight from foot to foot.
A quantum shift, maybe, but that was enough.
I loved her for it.

Today men gather to celebrate her sainthood.
Saint. Saint Lydia.
Ha! I can tell you she's no saint.
She's been with me more times than I can number.
I'll never forget how I slipped
between her thighs,
how her skin listened to all I had to tell it.
Yet she always kept me out,
just a little, a slight puff of space around her.

They did find the place where the current splits,
heads southward.
I run from the Pangaion,
source of all that is cold, clear, decent.
Now I hardly know myself
for all this stone and mortar.
Only men, I notice.
One wears a gold crown like an emperor,
gown embroidered with gold crosses.
Yet here the woman was baptized.
Here she would baptize others—
I can vouch for it—cup their heads in her palms,
release them to me.

Yet of all those delivered up,
she alone met me atom for atom, spark for spark.
As if I were husband,
as if I, a mere river, could satisfy her.
She was the one I wanted,
the only one I ever wanted back.

The Lydian Woman Speaks with the Pilgrim

"From now on, let no one make trouble for me;
for I carry the marks of Jesus branded on my body."
Galatians 6:17

Not so strange then for women—
there were plenty of us
all over the provinces.
Phoebe, oil—Corinth.
Prisca—tents.
I learned to bargain,
haggle the best prices,
call brokers by their first names,
remember the names
of their wives and children.
From here to the Black Sea,
the Dardanelles and beyond,
oxcart, donkey, grain-ship cargo,
wherever purple was worn.
Every sea-captain
proud to carry my purple.
Now I'm a tourist attraction.
Hotel Lydia!
Tourism's the thing here.
Converts. Conversion.
Convert souls. Convert currency.
The new baptistery beside
Lydia's River
kept up by the city of Kavala,
gaudy mosaics of Paul and me
over the doorway.

Euros pour in by the busload—
believers/non-believers,
what anyone wants everyone caters for.
One more prophet,
one more preacher—
there were scads of them
up and down the Aegean.
Paul. The brilliant market analyst.
Christ. A brand like Levi's.
It's all about drumming up business,
my husband used to tell me—getting out the word.

Philippi to Thyatira, November, 49 CE

"Who made you?
God.
What else did God make?
God made all things."
                     A Catechism for Young Children, #1, #2

"In the beginning was the Word, and the Word was with God,
and the Word was God."
                     John 1:1

Mother,
        Plague strangled us for months.
                         Spread up from Neapolis,
worse on the docks than anywhere else.
Now the hand lifts from Philippi's throat,
                     death's purse turns inside out.

       How I pitied him at the end. How glad I am he's gone.
Marriage a mantle I'd worn too long.

       My slaves no longer slaves—I freed them all.
We're a household. Four women, two boys.
Not one of us frightened.

       Every Sabbath we meet with Jews by the river.

       Yes, Mother, God. God has no body,
was born of no mother— no other before him,
                         not even himself.

God made the world from nothing,
nothing but words, so we are told, left it to his creatures.

God lives in high heaven, keeps his distance.
                                    How I welcome such a god!

      Much has happened since I boarded that boat from Troas.
Only fifteen!
More sadness I could not imagine.

                            Take these sesterces. Put them by.
Write to me, Mother. Let me know you are alive.

Thyatira to Philippi, Early March, 50 CE

Daughter,

        At long last, child. I'd given you up for dead.
Put stones at the foot of my mother's grave.
                                  I visit you daily.

        I hope this letter finds you in good health.
Tata told me to say that.
Tata studies books in a school the Romans built.
Tata writes down what I tell her.

        This sheet cost me dear.
My words look so small, like ants crawling to the edge
                              looking for a way off.

        The first words I've ever said not to vanish.

        But will they reach you, daughter?
The journey's hard even for papyrus.
                As long as I'm talking to you, you have breath.

        I think of your face as you hold this page,
your eyes on my words.

        You'd not know me, so stooped I've become.
The village looks after me,
keeps me in wood.

        To me you're still the girl who left.
                Now even your lettering has grown up.

A door in my heart had shut. Bolt fastened.
You open it, and with it, the pain.

I'm an old woman. You've broken her peace.

Now all I want is quiet.
Bed. Fire. Beans. Garlic.
Yet your words are proof. Proof I still have a daughter.

Philippi to Thyatira, Late March, 50 CE

"God is a dyer. As the good dyes which are called "true" dissolve with the things dyed in them, so it is with those whom God has dyed. Since his dyes are immortal, they become immortal by means of his colors. Now God dips what he dips in water."
The Gospel of Philip

"Seconds after this puncture, as the snail was expiring, a white mucus-like fluid was observed oozing out of the gland and, within a few minutes, a violet ink-like fluid began forming in the mixture."
Zvi C. Koren

    Mother!
I've never met a man like this—dyed with the spirit.
You know what it means
               for dye not to leave you.

    Not much of a man, really,
though of firm body,
        little hair to speak of.
        Not a man for women, I tell you that.

    But his voice! He says soon the world ends—
words so fervent I almost believe them.

    Four bolts to Seleucia, two to Alexandria,
one casket of purple arriving from Sidon.

                    For Rome we do our own dyeing.
That's how the man struck me
that morning at the river,
                    his life dyed with Christos.

    He beckoned us, one by one,
took our heads in his hands.
Light trembled on the water. I went under briefly.
                    In an instant I had gone from all time.

    Mother, you know how purple is made,
not inside the snail but outside it.

                    Without air and light
it could not happen.
                    We can never work our own redeeming.

                    Take these robes with you—
I said to them—living robes from a dead husband—
one for you, one for Silas.
You'll be glad for a change of linen.

    These men will get into scrapes like headlong children.

    The man's called Paulus. Yes, I'll say it—
when my heart opened,
more than God came in.
The man knows what he wants. For once it is not me.

Yes, I'm one of them now.
We meet in my shop before daybreak.

　　　Jesus. Christos.
Another young man dead—
but this one will return, not once every year like the others,
but once for all time.

　　　Think of it! To lose such a son
for the gift in his hands.
　　　　　　　　　If only I could love as he did.

　　　Soon it will be spring, time again for stirring.
Now more than ever, Mother, come!

The Lydian Woman Speaks with *Christianity Today*

No. Not a river but a fair stream.
The shock of it that morning.
That morning
I would have agreed to anything.
I had gooseflesh
before stepping in.
The voice. It was the voice—
from deep in the belly,
a cavern, steamy vein in rock.
No keening, no lamentation,
no blood drained in the temple,
only the hard waters of baptism.
Water cuts through rock,
cuts through everything.
A name tucked into my bosom
like a handkerchief of linen,
a name, not a hand.
New wine.
For this I'd need new skins.
Yes. The man came here. Left.
I said, stay. Take off your cloak,
Word-weary traveler,
strengthen your heart.
His face tanned leather
the color of his tents. He rarely
noticed what I was wearing.
This new linen tunic,
for example. Knife-pleats
the Ptolemies made famous.
Do you like it?

Mother warned me.
Take your goddesses with you.
Mother warned me.
Looks matter in a woman.
Paulus!
Never have I met a man more distracted
by what was not before him.
Did he even see me? Did he want to?

Thyatira to Philippi, August, 50 CE

    You ask me to pack up my belongings, sail for Neapolis.
You send sesterces enough for many crossings.

                                        It would kill me.
I do fine on my own just like I used to,
    only now use a cane a neighbor carved,
        painted birds on to make me feel like I'm flying.

I need more rest now is all.

        How can I leave River Lycus?
Stelae outside the village?
Those stones hold my dearest secrets. I tell them everything.

Tongues of our mothers live in the soil of Thyatira.
        Can I leave tongues still speaking?

        I'm accustomed to these grains and grasses,
wheat, barley, einkorn, millet.

            Stomach cannot convert at this late hour.
I need little but cheese, bread, yogurt,
    grains I know, greens I grow myself.

        No need to worry.
The gods are good and fruitful.
            Eggs from my hen-yard.
                    Milk from Mistress Ewe.
            Apples from the old tree you remember,
                              knotted worse than I am.

Nothing nothing is lacking dear daughter but you.

The Lydian Woman Speaks with a Buyer from Milan

"A single ounce of Tyrian dye required killing a quarter million snails; dyeing a single toga cost ten thousand snails alone."
>   Gastronomica: Journal of Food and Culture

Cross-dyed linen—ells of it.
Linen undyed. Cotton from Egypt.
Proud purple!
Sea-snails fished off the coast
of Sidon and Tyre
gave their lives for my purple.
Is that Armani you're wearing?
I like the cut.
Yes, here he sat.
Paul. Paul of Tarsus.
He brought us Jesus.
Jesus the Christ.
I said, bring him to my table.
A son is always welcome.
I know sons. How they rise
sleepy-brained, hair tossed,
sea-wrack, ocean,
how they cry for milk, fruit.
Later, women.
I'll show him my loom,
account books, accounting,
purple threads, purple in caskets,
bolts of cloth, not souls
for the tallying.

*Do we all need a reckoning,
a squaring of accounts?
I wished to believe all Paul taught us,
to take his words into my body—
blood-red, red-purple.
Unweave the weaver,
the weaver of words.
Souls rarely go away.
Look at mine, still stubbornly here,
still fully clothed, in a room
no longer a room, in a city
of broken columns, still taking and filling orders.*

Via Egnatia: A Road-Stone Speaks to the Pilgrim

"I am the way, and the truth, and the life. No one comes to the father except through me."
$$\text{John 14:6}$$

                        the ruins at Philippi

Nothing has changed, as they say, yet everything.
Now weeds grow over me. Once we stones were glorious.
We made empire happen. We go everywhere.
Or did. Even staying in place we all led to Rome.
Everybody, I mean *everybody,* came this way:
brigands, bandits, praetors, prefects, pilgrims,
crusaders, traders, sick people on litters,
letter carriers, slaves running away from their masters,
priests, preachers, teachers, students. Salves,
salvation, potions, penitent crosses, relics (lots of those),
gods of all shapes and sizes—everything for sale.
The world came to us. We could learn anything
we wanted without budging or opening a book.
Let me tell you—the gladiators were awesome.
So scantily clad! I'm a stone, a paver, a big slab of marble.
That doesn't mean I can't have feelings, does it?
Hunks, solid as rock. Boy, were those men buff.
Never owned their own lives—that's the sad part.
Always a bit downcast. I wanted to say, buck up,
you go into the coliseum. Fight. Show off your manhood.
And those little leather skirts you get to wear!
The soldiers were boring. Tins of water hanging
from their belts. Whining. Miss my wife,
miss my children. Empire. Shempire. Whose?
Not theirs. Injustice. Like that's new in the world.

A set-up, those matches. But, hey. We've all got our troubles.
I can't leave this road-bed, for example. See everything,
go nowhere.

> *I'm a member of the tribe of stones—*
> *the Way Imperial.*

Philippi to Thyatira, Late October, 50 CE

Mother,

    Nearly dawn when I write. I've not slept.
Members will come
                   before sun reddens the Pangaion.

    I've never stood before others like this,
all eyes on me.

    Even Isis altars are banished from houses.

    After everyone's gone, I'll climb the Acropolis,
sit on cool rock at the feet of Artemis,
a niche merely,
                   nothing grand like her temple at Ephesus.

    Paulus travels there soon for a mission among you.

                 Paulus. A man for all time.
Too great for his small frame.
Heart beats against bars of bone as if trying to get out.
He says the world ends, any day, any hour.
                          Belief gives him fire.

              I want to believe.

    That somewhere my dead son lives.
That I may see him, touch his brow to gauge the fever.

    We meet here every Sabbath.
God's son will save us.
No stones, no stelae,
               no confessing sins to a stone.

    Mother!
You sit in your hut out of pure stubbornness.
You can't stay bound to the past—new currents are stirring.

    Leave your weaving, your grains and grasses.
Leave those busy gods.
Why stay wedded to earth when God's in heaven?

    Your room is ready, passage certain.
No excuses—Mother—come!

The Lydian Woman Speaks with
The Christian Science Monitor

". . . color is what's left of life beyond forms, beyond truth or beliefs, beyond accepted joys and sorrows. Color . . . expresses our sexuate nature, that irreducible dimension of our incarnation."
          Luce Irigaray

I'm a woman, a woman of purple,
always too involved with the world
to seek the hereafter.
That morning the Word went in,
pricked the brain.
Changed forever,
forever not changed. Right here.
We met in my shop,
a tight little group
of Jesus followers.
I opened my house for worship,
liked the company.
No. No son, no daughter,
only a house, servants, business,
little to give me heart.
Pull up a stool. Draw close.
I can barely make out your features
in this dim light,
in this dim century.
What happened?
Then, hope of every stripe piped out
by every priest or priestess,
every roadside philosopher.

Now, muzak in every elevator,
in every hotel lobby.
How can you hear yourselves think?
At first, quiet talk.
A few hymns.
A small meal shared.
I made bread.
We read aloud letters
from brothers and sisters
on the road.
After Paul died his became priceless.

Philippi to Corinth, Early February, 51 CE

                House of Aquila and Prisca

Dear Paulus, brother,

    You left us in a high state. You. Silas.
I see you huddled before Prisca's brazier,
                        rubbing hands briskly.
A risk to sail in this weather. Though risk never stopped you.

    While your cloak hangs on its hook,
all seems easy.
                Belief fresh from the river.
            Shivers of elation among us that day, days after.
How to keep that up?

    I feel like the murex—crushed for its purple.
What I was, giving way to what I'm becoming.
                          Dark ledge, feet slipping.
I can't find purchase. Give me a hand.

    When you leave I'm on my own with others as lost as I am.

    Will God find me here among my servants—
no child, no husband,
                nothing but me and my purple?

    That Sabbath by the river.
Shock of cold. Old gods washing downstream.
Our walk back to the house,
        me in my shift, hair undone. How you laughed!

    Something happened. Just as you promised.
A lightness of heart—
the first since. . . . but you know about my boy.

    He would be twelve.
He'd help me in the business. Don't say wait for Jesus.
I want him. I need him now.

The Lydian Woman Speaks with the Pilgrim

You want clear? See this river.
Of course I wonder, like you,
like everyone.
That's the question, isn't it?
The one on everybody's mind?
Who saw him leave the tomb?
Not Paul, not Silas, nobody I knew.
Look. I grew up in Anatolia.
Cybele we called her.
Mother Goddess, Earth Mama.
My own mother dragged me
to every procession,
to every rite and ritual.
With Cybele and Attis it was theater.
After a week of fasting,
Attis rose up resurrected.
The lover/son was back!
As for Jesus, we're told,
he died, rose to heaven,
but nobody's seen him since.
Yes, I ran an assembly in my house.
But the first convert in Europe?
Conversion—not the word I'd use
for what happened here.
We just took on more gods—
up to a point.
Who has the best story?
Who touches the heart?
We called on the ones that worked
for us—at the time.

I saw another young man dead,
another mother lost and alone.
One woman,
one son,
one sorrow.
She weeps for all of us.
Mary, Mother of Jesus—
the only goddess we have left.

Corinth to Philippi, Late April, 51 CE

"Therefore, my dear friends, flee from the worship of idols."

". . . any woman who prays or prophesies with her head unveiled dishonors her head."

Corinthians   10:14; 11:5

Sister,

    Our assembly here is sparse, prone to seduction.

    Aphrodite. Aphrodite!

    Her temple sits on a hill, glitters to Cenchreae,
to Lechaeon, and beyond. In the streets,
                            in the marketplace,
scores of her priestesses
      in flimsy silks, thinnest linens,
                            anklets jangling,
hair down their backs like snowmelt on the Pangaion.

    How do we keep our eyes on the Word
with such flesh about?

    The wealthy have their ways, lord it over the others.
I left the church in Philippi in your hands. You—
more than anyone—
                smooth jagged tempers.

And sister. When Jesus comes, how will he find you? What will you be wearing?

Take these words into your bosom.

Be modest in your dress—the others will follow.

Your brother in Christ

Philippi to Corinth, June, 51 CE

"Paul . . . said to the Spirit, 'I order you in the name
of Jesus Christ to come out of her.'"
                                                    Acts 16:18

Paulus,

    You have stung my pride.
What business is it of yours what I wear or how I wear it?

                                    And, Paulus.
That slave-girl in town you thought
you cured of demons
                      merely worshiped Dionysus.
You took the child's tongue along with her living.
She had a gift. Read doom in my son's palm when he was a baby.

    Slaves have ways of shifting to make life barely tolerable.
What has she become?

    I know slaves, slave-hood. I know whoring.
My own earthly tent merely rented,
                      I never owned it.
          The old master first, then the young one.

    Yes. I grew up a slave in Lydia.
Stirred vats as a child, invited the whip if I stopped stirring.
        As I budded, got taller,
                the lash softened, lashes grew less frequent.

Believe me, I've paid for my freedom.

Once sold for silver, I now sell purple, buy what I choose.
Eat, drink, wear what I please.
Modesty's a luxury I can't afford.

And Paulus—you're in the city of Aphrodite.
The Word merely hovers at the mouth of her cave,
a frantic swallow.

Your sister in Christ

The Lydian Woman Speaks to the Dead Saint

". . . women should be silent in the churches. . . .
for it is a shame for a woman to speak in the church."
1 Corinthians 14: 34, 35

"In the world of Paul himself, we know that
the women were far from silent."
A. N. Wilson

The hate your words have engendered—
also love. A genius of hate
you've been called.
Also a genius of love. Sometimes
I hate your words!
More often love.
You speak of love with such feeling.
You hate whatever opposes you.
Dogs! Evil workers!
Words conceal/reveal.
Words revel in what they do not tell.
What is heaven
if not what you see before you?
River belongs to mountain,
sun to shadow,
swallow to air,
thistle to hillside.
Why beg God for grace
when we have grace already?
Wind blows down from the Pangaion.
A cold season.

Draw up a stool by the brazier.
This verse reversed your meaning.
Not yours. I knew it!
Paul. Brother. If only
you knew what has happened
to women
in your absence,
to the women you knew.
Your sisters written out of Scripture,
out of ritual, out of sacrament.
All, all in your name.

Thyatira to Philippi, Early September, 51 CE

"How long will you hide your face from me?"
          Psalm 13:1

"What is God?
God is a spirit, and has not a body like man."
          A Catechism for Young Children, #9

     Beetles have got into our elms—beetles a pestilence
like Rome.

     So this God of Israel has a son.
Why not a daughter?
              She'd bleed with us every moon,
       that would be some comfort.

And this Paulus. Not the first voice you've fallen for, daughter!
Take care where heart goes.

     Rome swarms the fields.
Rome piles up stones to the emperor, his likeness everywhere.

     Rome swallows the countryside.
     Rome takes the best wheat, leaves us vetch and darnels.

Rome comes with a new kind of hunger,
                       that of a wolf set out to starve.

Do you have wolves where you are?

    Can your god save a child?
Apollo himself came to our village. Did not send his son
or anyone else to do it.
              We have eyewitnesses.

    A god of no body, yet a father.
Does your god sport in water? Does he know how to dance,
pipe tunes naked in a grove,
                          make love under a mountain?

    Never trust a god, daughter,
who cannot or will not lose himself in a woman.

The Lydian Woman Speaks to the Dead Saint

"How can we dwell on earth without goddesses?"
                                        Luce Irigaray

Always the same colors, the same weather.
Words start, startle into being.
Keep skins from tearing.
Word opens, woman enters.
Will Word close up over her?
A woman speaks through every opening.
Until gods bathe with goddesses
a woman has no tongue.
Woman at the belly of creation
pushed to its outskirts.
If only you were here,
if only you could see me now.
You would be welcome—Paul!
But no welcome at all
for that flat-footed God
who would not embrace Woman
in her streaming abundance.
Seasonless god/single parent.
What manner of man
comes through woman,
neither needing her, nor cherishing?
You said follow. I did.
Was your God ever ready
for such as woman, woman
as she strides over,
straddles mountain?
Can your God
receive her/conceive of her?

Asherah! Asherah!
Did El put you away?
Send you back to your own people?
How did you offend?
Was it your blood?
Too much the odor of birth?
Night's blade swings swiftly down,
brings day's circumcision,
day drowns in purple.
A woman need not be cut to bleed.

Philippi to Thyatira, March, 52 CE

"For as often as you eat this bread and drink this cup,
you proclaim the Lord's death until he comes."
$$\text{1 Corinthians 11:26}$$

Mother,

    Wine first? Or bread?
Syntyche says this, Euodoia that.
House splits down the middle,
        each Sabbath each faction louder,
            more vehement.

        Body of Christ!
Was his blood spilled for this?
We argue rather than eat,
        the bread lead on my stomach.

    Business suffers, orders back up.
I lie awake nights.

    Only Paulus brings order.
        My voice is small, my words borrowed
from the man who brings them up Via Egnatia
    like rolls of leather or bolts of linen
    to receive the precious dye stored in a casket.

Will these words ever become mine—
with my own tincture and feeling?
If God sent his son to bring peace,
                                        surely God is failing.

                    Purple belongs to Paulus.
He journeys. We fall to dissension.

       Mother—tell me—what's to save us from ourselves?

The Road-Stone Speaks to the Pilgrim

I heard everything. Like the old ones chanting down the road
long before they got to my station. All jazzed about
the soul's migration, soul showing up in a blade of grass,
a sheep or a goat, a cricket or a cat. *Why slaughter
a bull-calf, why slaughter kin, why slaughter a bull-calf,
you may come back as one.* Souls come, souls go.
Never light for long anywhere. The souls I've known
on this worn carcass! Their followers, once tagging behind,
now out front, big as life. They said the soul's
immortal, scratched little proofs on our mileposts.
Which I resent. But I pitied them from my heart.
They couldn't step for stumbling, tripping on their shoelaces,
necks craned upward. What's underfoot is not real.
Not my ideas! I'm just passing them along.
Those after the stumblers jeered at them, threw rocks
at women. Said the soul dies with the body.
That's that. End of story. Some sourpusses brought their dogs
with them. By Jove, I love the talk, but hate being pissed on!
Some thought they knew everything.
Others knew nothing. Everyone getting into the act.
Everyone going somewhere. Some walked
ramrod straight, spouted Moderation. Others—
stuff your gullet, soon you're dust anyway. I say—
live and let live, let people believe whatever they like.
If I could eat well, sleep out of the weather, you can bet I'd do it.

We'd get people where they needed to go.

The Lydian Woman Speaks with *Ms. Magazine*

"I have suffered the loss of all things, and do count them but dung that I may win Christ."
						Philippians 3:8

"In those days you would have been hard put to find anyone who believed in 'sexual equality' in the modern sense, and the person who comes closest to it is, strangely enough, Paul."
						A. N. Wilson

Yes, I knew Paulus.
Or Paul as he's now called.
He came, went, wrote rarely.
That I cannot answer.
Though once he did tell me
he had a wife Hannah,
she got sick in the womb,
died with the baby.
That made him wander,
that made him angry with God.
Nor can you take literally
all that you read,
his words twisted by those
coming after him.
At first Paul seemed
a new sort of man,
one who listened beyond
what I said
to what I was saying.
Some say he hated the world.

Never satisfied
is how I remember him,
always thirsting
for something not there.
I only wish he could have
enjoyed life a bit more,
taken the world more as he found it.
But you would like him.
Everyone did.
With all his talk of heaven
he's the only man on earth
who ever made me feel truly alive.

Philippi to Ephesus, April, 52 CE

" . . . . not alone at Ephesus, but almost throughout all Asia,
this Paul has persuaded and turned away many people, saying
that they be no gods, which are made with hands."
Acts 19: 26

Paulus,

     Another riot narrowly avoided!
Must you bait the officials, ask for trouble like a wayward boy?

     Folks don't give in easily.
Just look at my mother—childhood gods deep-dyed within her.
Do look in on her.
              Thyatira—only days away from Ephesus.

     In her youth, all color and noise.
Loved showy things, good theater. The more gods the better!

     Paulus—
          you've stepped onto the soil of the great Artemis.
Many-breasted,
all-powerful mother. If you sat on her lap, drank
           from her paps,
           would you be filled with longing?
Thirst so for a world to come?

                              In Ephesus,
the Nazarene's an upstart, mere stripling,
wet behind the ears.
            No pedigree, no sanctuary. No grove, cave, river.
            No rock-face niche for votives.

    If you refuse to pay homage to their goddess,
you'll be brushed off like a mosquito
                        in the swamp,
no more listened to than a frog belching its story.

    Faith slips through my fingers like water. Paulus!
You escape the daily business of the *ekklesia*.
            Bread. Bowls. Fish carted over from Neapolis.
Who are the hangers on? Who of the faith?
            All have to eat.

    Members still quarrel. Bread, wine. Wine, bread.
Can it matter to God?
Paulus—are we such fallen creatures that love comes this hard?

The Lydian Woman Speaks with the Pilgrim

"Perhaps I'll rewrite my own story. Delete the silences,
the hesitations, the shrinking from life."
The Pilgrim

What's your pleasure?
To know more? To know me?
The man came here. Left.
I have been known
far too often. Have known
far too many stories.
Knowing me will not save you.
Your story is your own.
Love? In love with Paulus?
Love, as you call it—
not the way things worked.
To move up,
a woman married.
My master became my husband.
He gave me a son,
gave me my freedom.
Freedom for little but bed
and business. Still—
I was better off than most.
Yes, I was good to look at.
Skin dark. Eyes black.
Bosom ample. Ample hips.
I walked about in white wool,
never wore the purple I sold.
It was far too costly.

When sun blares along Via Egnatia,
what's left of it,
I still walk up the Acropolis
to caves, stone carvings.
Diana/Artemis.
Cybele/Mother.
Yes, my husband hit me.
Even during lovemaking.
Sometimes I liked it.
Needle's eye, I would pass through it.
I have earned every drachma.

Thyatira to Philippi, Late October, 52 CE

Daughter,

    Hens are not laying. No eggs for weeks.
                         Past season for apples.
Worst drought in years. The countryside suffers.

    Those meetings—does Jesus himself come?
Where's cymbal, tambourine, zither?
              How can you bear the talk? I'd want to dance.

    Do you serve the buns I taught you?
Cloves, nutmeg, cinnamon.
        Remember with cardamom always a light hand.
Don't stint on wine.
    Mix it with honey. You can afford it.
                Sweeten life when you can.

    Bones are weak, eyes cloudy. Tata stays
most nights, sleeps on a straw pallet, keeps a fire going.

    I think of you still sleek and beautiful,
running your business.
Every sesterce counted, every sesterce accounted for.

    And yet you skulk among Jesus followers.
A poor lot who mean to stay poor!
You know better than go about in tatters.
                    That much I've taught you.

  Hold onto your money, that's your freedom.
Feed fear to the jackals,
       or love won't come in.
Be a slave to no one, not even your Christos.

  When Jesus comes back will he know me?
When Jesus comes back will he dance like Dionysus?
When Jesus comes back what will he bring us?
Here we need bread.

Philippi to Ephesus, March, 53 CE

"Let this mind be in you, which was also in Christ Jesus. . . who, emptied himself, taking the form of a slave. . . and became obedient to the point of death."
        Philippians 2:5-8

"Good women are obedient. They guard their unseen parts because God has guarded them. As for these whom you fear for disobedience, admonish them and send them to beds apart and beat them."
        Quran 4:34

Paulus,

  To know you're alive, safe—though in prison.

  I send back blankets, herbs to cool the fever,
linen tunic, not new but just laundered,
leather belt, a pair of sandals—the last of my husband's—never worn,
    and likely to fit
      though he was taller than you by a hand-width.

  Your words strike the quick of my heart.
Do nothing rash!
    You've enemies enough without becoming your own.

  Would you make mourners of your friends?

  On second thought, I leave out the belt.
Let Jesus wait! We welcome Timotheus with all our hearts.
    But it's you we long for.

I can't sleep for thinking. Paulus—
such a hard thing you ask of us.
> To obey you as Jesus obeyed his Father. *Obedience.*
> A word too familiar for comfort.

Obedience—once posted to the blood—
is all but impossible to purge. It seeps into the skin,
> under the nails like dye.
> Had I been bound to obedience, I'd still be a slave in Thyatira.

Have you brought coin in the marketplace?
> Watched your mother forced? Father beaten?
You, Paulus, neither slave nor woman.

Come back—don't delay your journey.
My cat Gratia will kiss your hand if you let her,
> her kiss holy as any other.

Can we not work out our salvation with joy?

Your sister in Christ

Ephesus to Philippi, Late April, 53 CE

"For the wisdom of the world is foolishness with God."
$$\text{1 Corinthians 3:19}$$

Dear Sister,

    Calm yourself!
        I've no intention of unhanding my own life.

            Believe me,
I would be there if I could.
As to Eudoia and Syntyche—
        I trust you not to let the rift widen.

    Bread broken.
        Vine drunk. In that order.

    Not Osiris. Not Attis. Not Dionysus.
            But Jesus the Christ.

    Still, such notions may be hard to swallow.

    As to your other point, you miss my meaning.
We can't be like the others.
We must set ourselves apart from the world.

    World. What is found there?
Virtue lashed for disobeying those who eat on gold plates.

    Clatter of gold in the marketplace,
in the coffers of monarchies and republics. Gold.

A world turned upside down, backwards,
must be shocked into rightness.

    Creditor. Debtor. What does it matter?
        Jesus awaits—
                    the only coin worth having.

Paulus

The Lydian Woman Speaks to the Dead Saint

"For we know that if the earthly tent we live in is destroyed, we have a building from God, a house not made with hands, eternal in the heavens. For in this tent we groan, longing to be clothed with our heavenly dwelling."
                                        2 Corinthians, 5:1-2

Your tents. Your tent of flesh.
Your words/your purple
spun into doctrine
still sold in the marketplace.
Bibles abound.
Best selling book.
Heaven's for real.
On sale here. 12.95 USD.
christiansupply.com.
Every room in every motel
has its own Gideon.
The Word a salve,
a stinging nettle.
Will I be unsaid by it?
Will I be found unworthy?
Scholars spend their lives
explaining you,
the Word/your words
their living.
Words hovering,
words hover above meaning,
will not land.
Day bleeds on the mountain.
Bleeds.

What Yahweh once wanted.
Blood. Flesh.
Was pleased/not pleased
by the odor of offal, of fat smoking.
He sent his son, his only.
I too had a son. He was six.
Fever breeds in the marshes.
Silphium alone relieves it.
The boy I thought
destined for legions
destined for a jar. Buried here.
Did God decide I'd had him long enough?

Philippi to Caesarea, Prison, December, 57 CE

"I fed you with milk . . . for you were not ready for solid food."
                                          1 Corinthians 3:2

Paulus,

    Once more you've left—you, Timotheus—
bright spots in an otherwise bleak season.
                                  Winds hard from the sea.
                  Wise not to land now.

    Cold settles on the plain, snow on the Pangaion
a cloak of undyed linen.
            Lavinia keeps embers going, yet hands stay cold.

    Summer baptism.
Not indoors like so often now,
                        a jar of water dumped on the head.
You laugh as you read this,
        stretched out on your stone bed,
                stone for a head-pillow. My soft life!

    Two dozen bolts of my best woolen just left
by cart for Neapolis. With luck,
the wind at its back, the ship will get to Rome in two months.
                    Yes,
        I've been paid by the middle-dealer.
              Else I'd not survive in this business in such weather.

    Do you total up souls like bolts of linen?

    Paulus—
you speak to us as children, yourself as nursing mother.
        Breasts filling, emptying—
            can you know how that feels? Emptying, filling—
not for the world but for this child. This child.

Your sister who tries to be faithful, the way you taught it

The Road-Stone Speaks to the Pilgrim

A fellow came over us, weary, yet he did not seem burdened
like so many others. I'm worn down by wayfarers,
most of them forgotten. This one I remember
by his light tread, despite what he carried.
Awl. Hammer. Rolls of leather strapped to his back.
One of many swarthy travelers. Nobody
would've looked at him twice but for the voice.
Jesus. Jesus the Christ. His Way the only. And only
for those who believe. That's what the man said.
He came through more than once. Brought
others with him. This Way goes to some kingdom
you can't see but know when you get there.
No mileposts or marble pavers. His followers,
now plentiful as donkeys, never saw eye to eye.
*He's God in a human body. No, only a man,
it's the Christ in us that matters.* Mud. Dust. Frost.
Wet. Have we been through it! Thieves.
They'd steal anyone blind. Guards patrolling the road.
Half on the take, the other half crazy.
This God-forsaken hole. Believe me,
we've seen it all. Know what it amounts to.
Killing, looting, old skins, old bottles.
Human waste, wasted humans. Sometimes all I want
is a good washing. To be a clean river stone, small and useless.

The way to heaven? Don't ask me!

The Lydian Woman Speaks to the Dead Saint

"Who can find a virtuous woman? For her price is far above rubies."
Proverbs 31:10

Day goes down, beds with ocean,
throws off her purple.
Day ends as woman.
You invited us to speak.
You said—sisters, work with us.
Will your God ever clasp us
to his bosom,
weep with us by the river?
Does your god ever weep?
Sky rolls up like a scroll.
Eye of purple, eye of world.
I'd ask, does the Word
get heavy on your back?
Strings tied, bolts bundled, trundled
aboard the latest grain-carrier.
No middleman, no broker
for this faith, this purple.
I watch for the flash of purple,
never weary of it.
Hear the hum? Hum deepest in?
Even now you can hear it.
Every thread,
every filament
vibrates with being.

Is faith mere obedience,
merely taking the word of others?
Faith a weapon,
faith a bludgeon—
if not yours, someone else's?
You said, empty yourself, sister.
Let Christ come in.
Time's no arrow
but a blind worm inching forward.
I have been here. Still am.

Rome to Philippi, May, 60 CE

"And so we came to Rome."   Acts 28:14

                    Tanning Yard at the Tiber

Grace and Peace.

                          Rome—Sister!
Poor creatures fallen on false gods.

    Streets filled with dust. Carts. Dung. Donkeys.
Hawkers. Magicians. Jugglers. Fortune-tellers.
    Colored silks. Silver jewelry.
                Trash. Trinkets.
Such a lot of bewildering glitter.
                    Tents. Shoes of leather.
                    Parchment. Almond paste. Pastries.

    Buying. Selling. Selling. Buying. On every corner.
Noise. Confusion. Rattle of wheels
so insistent they're banned sunup to sundown.

    The emperor. A parody of himself,
parody of emperor.
A god—he tells them—what a god.
A god who takes, gives little.
            Flings grain to the people, parades in a gold chariot.

Junia and Andronicus have been here for some time.
They knew Jesus.

    Junia! Clear mind, generous heart. She argues me down—
point for point. I love her for it. Andronicus,
a modest man who says little. Worthy helpmeet.

    Junia! Strong in the faith, yet she questions everything.
Knows when to ask—when to leave off.

    Take lightly your life in the Lord—dear sister—
                             be ready to give it up in a twinkling.

Paulus

The Lydian Woman Speaks to the Dead Saint

"There is neither Jew nor Greek, there is neither bond nor free, there is neither male nor female: for you are all one in Christ Jesus."
Galatians 3:28

No longer on your travels,
you've taken up residence
in chapter and verse,
your words on the tongues
of men and women,
your words no longer your own.
Come in by the fire.
You welcomed us. You did.
You said you heard
Jesus in the road.
Did you beget your own savior?
New promise.
New creation.
When if ever do we stop waiting?
The Church failed you.
Phoebe you called deacon.
Junia you called foremost
among the apostles—
Junia/Junias/Junia—
named and unnamed sisters
tossed on the bone-heap.
Had Jesus been a woman,
not God's son
but God's daughter,
would you have preached her?

*Cramp in the belly,
pain in the side—
not once and it's over,
sacrifice done,
but once every moon
death sheds its skin.
Would you have deemed
her blood glorious,
childing a worthy sacrifice?*

Philippi to Rome, January, 61 CE

"He lived there two whole years at his own expense and welcomed all who came to him..."
	Acts 28:30

"The lictors clear a path for it, and purple indicates the dignity of boyhood. It distinguishes senators from knights, and is summoned to appease the gods."
	Pliny the Elder

Paulus,

    Are you still in chains? A guard always with you?

    I've sold more to Nero than any before him.
Finest purple. Finest finish.
No single stripe, either. He lavishes purple about wildly,
                            wants whole cloaks of it.

    The waters of Sidon and Tyre exhausted
from his orders alone. Chests filled
                      with purple wool
            embroidered with silver and gold thread—
sun, moon, stars. Emperor of the universe!
So he believes.

    My mother died in her sleep last month.
At peace, they tell me.

    Will I ever again see her or my son?
Would God in His Heaven
              keep out an ignorant old woman
                                and a dead boy?
Others are asking.

    What's rare is valued—Paulus—
        purple crushed from a tiny mollusk, your friendship—
I can't live without it.

Rome to Philippi, April, 61 CE

                House of Junia and Andronicus
                Transtiberinum

Sister,

    Paulus may be proudest of your church. Credits you
        with its sweetness.
                And resilience.
Worries about you like a brother, more than a brother,
had he not taken a vow.

    We all know the story. Damascus Road
after the crucifixion. He saw a light. Heard a voice.
                        Maybe he did.
Such has not happened to me.
Nor to Andronicus. Nor to anyone else here.

    I will say this. We saw Jesus alive.
In Galilee. Awesome man. Whether he rose from the dead,
whether he'll return, I can't tell you.

    While he was here, he had throngs calling out his name,
tearing his garments.
Jews mostly, a few Gentiles. Weeping, laughing.

    There we sat on a sultry day in mid-summer,
gathered to hear the prophet.
        Not the thousands talked of later,
                still a goodly number.
Astonishing, I said to Andronicus, how he moves the crowd.

No charlatan, no magician. Merely a young Galilean
in a ragged robe. Later we heard stories—
> how loaves and fishes multiplied miraculously.

I happen to know, firsthand,
> women of the village baked that bread,
> men of the village caught those fish.
> > Fresh mullets—delicious!

Junia

The Lydian Woman Speaks to the Dead Saint

"In a moment, in the twinkling of an eye, at the last trump: for the trumpet shall sound, and the dead shall be raised incorruptible, and we shall be changed."
        1 Corinthians 15:52

"It's a beautiful night for a rapture."
        International Herald Tribune, May 23, 2011

SAVE THE DATE. MAY 21, 2011.
REPENT! JESUS IS COMING SOON.
Media blitz in Oakland.
Billboards.
Millions of pamphlets.
Some quit their jobs in anticipation.
You'd be grave, then amused.
You'd say they missed the point.
Has the Galilean
already returned—
as a Galileo or an Einstein?
You must've known
everything you said
could not be treated as gospel.
How will I meet him?
As an old woman,
dry riverbed, no springs left,
yellow hills, parched grasses?
Or in my new making
will Jesus take me backwards,
love's loins untried, untested?
Back of the white shift—blood.

*A girl quakes to be
found out, discovered.
Her sin—womanhood.
Shame. I will not take it.
No shame before Jesus.
Will breasts fallen
rise like loaves to greet him?
Here I'll be sitting,
last bolt unrolled, unfolded,
warp and weft tightly woven,
not a single thread missing.
When will Jesus come for his cloth?*

Rome to Philippi, August, 61 CE

"Let anyone among you who is without sin be the first
to throw a stone at her."
$$\text{John 8:7}$$

                House of Junia and Andronicus
                Transtiberinum

Sister,

      The marshes are virulent. Dog Days, they call them.
Few breezes, if any.

      Our numbers are swelling. Jews. God-fearers.
Romans of no clear stripe or faith—curious mostly.
                      This Way of Life the new contagion.

      As for me, Jesus is no apparition, no voice in the road.

      Will he come back as promised? All I can tell you—
if Jesus does return, he has heart enough
to take us all in. Even women.
                    Women especially.

      Andronicus and I were there that day outside the temple,
           all shouting: Adulteress, adulteress.
                    Stone her, stone her.
Jesus went to her. Held out his hand.
      The woman raised her head, face bruised, shift dirtied.

>   She said nothing, just edged away,
> touching no one, no one touching her.
>   The circle widened like water disturbed by a stone.
>   The crowd widened to let her through.
>
>   We travelled the Aegean twenty winters
> before settling in Rome. Exhausted. Needed to land.
>
>   We were not at the Crucifixion. Who could bear it?
> We met Paulus soon after. Fell in with him
>   for a while. In prison together. In chains.
>
>   A woman's necessary business is not a man's.
> Let's just say we've been through it.
> I feel like his sister.
>   Always will.
>
>   Right away I was impressed by his zeal.
> And a bit scared. I'd tell him—man-meteor—you'll turn to ash.
>
>   He hates with such brilliance. And loves!

Your sister in Christ,

Junia

The Lydian Woman Speaks to the Dead Saint

". . . suddenly a light from heaven flashed around him."
                                          Acts 9:3

Photons/light bundles.
A vision. Light blunders.
What if those particles of light,
those waves of sound,
met someone else
in Damascus Road—
someone with no gift for language,
or otherwise engaged.
It is said, you cared
not a fig for the living Jesus.
It is said, you made up
the Christ you wanted.
Day bleeds in the west,
sparks/splash/splay of photons,
quarks unleashed.
Word made flesh.
Whose word?
Word curled up like a cat.
A point hot, black,
a dot infinitesimal, infinite,
cooled, uncurled
to make a world.
Does time make ripe,
rip the fabric?
End of time—end of a string,
a ball of yarn unwinding.

*Were you here now
would you probe the shaft
of the cosmos,
de-robe it with equations
until it stood bare,
star-struck, shining?
In the beginning the Word.
The Word a mote,
remote in earliest universe.
Time smeared, spread out,
stained purple
like paramecia under a microscope,
iodine on a wounded finger.*

Rome to Philippi, May, 62 CE

Sister,

    The Tiber stinks with hate.
            Our meeting place changes from Sabbath to Sabbath.

    In Christ—you ask.
To die. Die to the old life, come back renewed, refreshed—
              I almost said refleshed—
which may be nearer the truth. I'm out of my depth.

    The rest I leave to Paulus.
I love the man, love his mind. He's no slave to the literal.
        Sometimes my head spins so I miss his meaning.

    I say let words go! I do know this—
the heart needs a good cleaning, inside out, cobwebs
swept, new mats laid down.
            Not only the hearts of others,
but ours too, ours especially. That I fathom.

    As for the world to come, why speak of it?
Much to do here.

    Nero—worse than any before him. One who kills his mother—
wicked as she was—will do anything.
        Even the Senate's bewildered.
Wives. Poisonings. Palaces.
    No stopping his excesses. And so many starving!

Danger increases daily.
Tell me—how can God's children become so distant from God?

Junia

The Lydian Woman Speaks with a Supplier from Cairo

". . . when thine eye is single, thy whole body also is full of light."
$\qquad$ Luke 11:34

"Lo, I, a woman in front of all! Behold this male child!"
$\qquad$ The Burden of Isis

Isis. Isis of the lapis eye, once all the rage
in Philippi. That was then.
Few have heard of her now.
She came from Egypt on bales
of linen, of cotton.
Cotton carried her.
Came with large-mouthed dealers
bringing cloth to market.
Her brother/husband
lost in fragments on the Delta.
Her son Horus on her lap
like Mary's son Jesus.
Osiris. Attis. Dionysus. Jesus.
Must all gods be eaten?
Must all men be wept over?
Hope rises after a night of wailing,
hope comes with exhaustion.
Day opens its one spent eye.
Live rock, living water.
We still worship the invisible.
We plumb the depths of creation
with numbers,
would find its single eye.

Dionysus, first love,
came to my pillow.
Every love a failure.
Every love a story.
Mine—I will not tell it.
Eye of agate, eye of lapis,
golden thighs, bones of silver.
Will he bring bread of the whitest flour?
Will he bring bread?
Is belief a door opening and closing?
Is belief a window shuttered tight?

The Lydian Woman Speaks to the Dead Saint

"In the beginning was not the Word. In the beginning was the hearing."

                                  Nelle Morton

In the beginning not a name
but a hum.
Threads on a loom,
no name to believe
or not to believe in.
Instead of belief a listening.
Hum beyond hearing.
Strings of time
strumming down darkness.
Is God the one above all
who listens?
Names come, names go.
Not even purple
finds its way here,
soaks into threads
at their own deepest humming.
Luke says light blinded you.
You fell down before it.
Is it always light
unmans/emasculates?
Can dark also do it?
Holy wave. Holy particle.
Are the blind best at seeing?
Is belief a bargaining?
Submit. Submit.
He said: come here.

He said: loosen your girdle,
let down your hair.
Dare you commend slavishness
even to God, to Jesus?
Can one base act bring redemption?
Must I believe
in someone else's vision,
fall down before it?
The cosmos—a reckoning.
Starting now.
The cosmos deserves dearest light.

Philippi to Rome, Early April, 63 CE

                    House of Junia and Andronicus

Dear Junia,

    How our brother Paulus stays on the mind—
how I want him to return,
                    how I want him not to.

    You'd think he owned the place!
Servants and all.
What's for supper, dear Sister?
                          He heads for the kitchen.

    He'd curb festivals in Philippi,
                  or worse, have me do it.

    Dionysus, we're told, born at the foot of the Pangaion.
Everyone turns out for his procession—
        including women of my household.
I go with them. And why not?

    I love the man like a brother, long for his presence.
But after two days I wish him gone.
Sister—
        I no longer feel Christos in my body.
Should I?
                Tear up this letter when you have read it.

Your Sister

Rome to Philippi, June, 63 CE

". . . but I see another law in my members, warring against the law in my mind. . . Wretched man that I am! Who will rescue me from the body of this death?"
                              Romans 7:23, 24

        House of Junia and Andronicus
        Transtiberinum

Sister,

    Our Paulus fights cult as he fights everything. Especially his own urges.
                This is Rome!
        Rome, I tell him.
                Romans will have their pleasure.

    All the while need groans in the gutter,
                shows its face in every alley.

    Need scratches its name on the roadside.

    Need appears at every market.

    Need cries out to the emperor—is not heard.

        Need, sickly, covered in scabs, darts into Via Sacra, restless and scrawny as hungry cats.

    I know my calling.
It has little to do with the Word, less to do with Paulus.

Yet this Way of Life grows wider,
                                our numbers increase daily.

Think of us—Sister. Pray for our safety.

Yours in Christ,

Junia

Ostia to Philippi, Late August, 64 CE

"Some were covered with the skins of wild beasts, and left to be devoured by dogs; others were nailed to the cross; and many covered over in inflammable matter, were lighted up, when the day declined, to serve as torches in the night."
$\qquad\qquad\qquad\qquad\qquad$ Tacitus

Dear Brothers and Sisters of Philippi,

$\qquad$ By now you've heard. Paulus likely dead.

$\qquad$ Not a month since a spark flew up near the Circus.
Anything could have started it,
$\qquad\qquad$ so dry these hills.

$\qquad$ I'd set out for market as usual.
Heard a dry rumbling.
As if every cart trundled through streets after hours.

$\qquad$ Then silence. Sky dyed red.
Ash rained for days. Even pines on the Aventine blackened,
their pitch like tinder.

$\qquad$ Surely we welcomed the fire, if we did not start it.

$\qquad$ Transtiberinum.
Paulus. Junia. Andronicus. Everyone, everyone taken.

$\qquad\qquad\qquad\qquad$ Even the children.
Loaded screaming into wagons.
Their belongings left behind.

When Nero's men came looking we were in Ostia.
          Had blended in. Safe for now.
                        Sail soon to Cenchreae.

I'm glad you're far far from Rome. May you never go there.

Your sister in Christ,

Prisca

The Lydian Woman Speaks to the Pilgrim

"And the Word was made flesh, and dwelt among us."
$\qquad\qquad\qquad$ John 1:14

"Read this Book and rely on it, and you will always lead
a sweet Christian life."
$\qquad\qquad\qquad$ To the pilgrim from her grandmother,
$\qquad\qquad\qquad$ Easter Sunday, 1957

Spacetime stretches
like good linen when wet.
The words in red—are they His?
Blood on these pages.
Red-ink savior.
I miss festivals. Blood.
Sometimes even my own.
Spacetime a mere fabric
the sun rolls in.
Ether. Ozone. Planet.
Purple needs no atonement.
Purple needs no redeeming.
Red/violet, red/purple
never lost to the fleece
that soaks it up.
Abram. Abraham!
Why so ready with the knife?
No woman I know
would take a blade
to her young son's throat,
wait for God to snatch it.

*When is it faith,
when a mere gamble?
My first fruit, my only.
Lines in his palm spelled doom
from the beginning,
his childhood short as a taper.
Had he known Jesus,
water poured over his body,
would the fever have left him?
Will my words become his flesh,
my prayer his presence?
I think of Mary and weep.
Will every mother's son rise up blessed?*

The Road-Stone Speaks to the Pilgrim

Then, we went all the way from Dyrrachium to Byzantium,
Dürres to Istanbul, if you've checked a recent map.
Now, cast aside for scrap, curiosity seekers. For tourists
to gape at, flip out iPhones to take photos of.
One of the oldest roads in the world. Blah, blah, blah.
But I can tell you, once upon a time, we *worked.*
Felt every wheel, every hoof, every tail of every lash
striking every back. I still love clear nights—
stars tossed like trinkets in the vast bowl of sky
when the young come to try out their bodies.
You should've seen me and my mates fresh from the quarry.
Pristine. Virginal. Straight out of that mountain.
Now everyone's practically naked. Speak in fragments.
Ride bicycles, bring water bottles, roll strollers over us.
Scrolls in knapsacks. Books in backpacks, on Kindles.
You'd think by now words would be worn out.
Papyrus wears thin, paper tears apart. One blink,
the screen goes blank. What stands the test of time?
Stone. What you're walking on. We'll be here
long after you and your words are gone. Once we stones
were glorious, the weight of empire upon us.
We moved troops, merchants; odd gods, odd notions.
That tentmaker was not the first to talk about Jesus,
to spread the Word, as he called it. Nor the last,
that's for damn sure. Like I've always known, whatever Rome
gets behind thrives. If anything on earth is eternal, it would be stone.

The way to heaven? Don't ask me!

The Lydian Woman Speaks to the Dead Saint

*Antioch. Seleucia.
Salamis. Paphos.
Perga in Pamphylia.
Antioch in Pisidia.
Iconium. Lystra.
Derbe. Attalia.
Troas. Neapolis.
Philippi. Amphipolis.
Apollonia. Thessalonica.
Beroea. Athens.
Corinth. Ephesus.
Caesarea. Rome.
You know where you've been.
You dragged the Word
to Kingdom Come and back.
You gathered up
this patchwork of empire—
the Word your needle—
stitch by tiny stitch,
delivered it one smooth fabric,
one Christ-dyed garment,
first to the Emperor,
then to the Pope.
As always, I'm ready to see you,
my sandals oiled,
a fresh linen tunic,
stola of new wool.*

*Though I can never predict
your coming, I plant myself beside
the forum entrance,
ramp of grooved marble,
lines like scripture.
Jesus has not come back
as you promised.
Many are still waiting.
I am not one of them,
though I still watch for you swinging your bundle
over Via Egnatia and through Neapolis Gate.*

Notes

Page 5: Scholars consider the entire passage in Acts, particularly 16:40, as evidence of a "house church assembly" in Lydia's house, Lydia at its head. The verse reads: "And they went out of the prison, and entered into the house of Lydia: and when they had seen the brethren, they comforted them, and departed." See Osiek and Macdonald, *A Woman's Place: House Churches in Earliest Christianity* (Minneapolis, 2006), 158. For the Greek terms "theosebes" and "sebomene," I am indebted to Stephen Mitchell's *Anatolia: Land, Men, and Gods in Asia Minor,* Vol. 2 (Oxford, 1993), 31-32.

Page 10: The centennial celebration of Lydia's sainthood took place beside the Gangites in Philippi on May 21, 2011.

Page 12: For the notion of Paul as entrepreneur and Jesus as a brand, I am indebted to Robert Wright, "One World, Under God," *The Atlantic* (April 2009), 40. The city of Kavala was called "Neapolis" in 1st century CE.

Page 13: As Lawrence F. Cunningham reminds us: "at the start of his Gospel, John consciously alludes to the creation account in Genesis." ("The New Testament" in *The Norton Anthology of World Religions*, ed. Jack Miles, New York, 2015, 802).

Page 17: "The Gospel of Philip," *Nag Hammadi Library: The Definitive New Translation of the Gnostic Scriptures, Complete in One Volume,* ed. James M. Robinson (San Francisco, 1978), 146. Recent production of the dye is described by Zvi C. Koren in "The First Optimal All-Murex All-Natural Purple Dyeing in the Eastern Mediterranean in a Millennium and a Half" in *Dyes in History and Archeology* 20, 140.

Page 24: Jude Stewart, "Cooking Up Color," *Gastonomica; The Journal of Food and Culture,* Fall 2011, 56.

Page 30: Luce Irigaray, *je, tu, nous: Toward a Culture of Difference,* trans. Alison Marten (New York, 1993), 109.

Page 40: "genius of hate": Harold Bloom quotes Nietzsche's *The Antichrist:* "Paul is the incarnation of a type which is the reverse of that of the Savior; he is the genius in hatred, in the standpoint of hatred, and in the relentless logic of hatred." *Genius: A Mosaic of One Hundred Exemplary Creative Minds* (New York, 2002), 140. "This verse reversed your meaning." 1 Corinthians 14: 34-35 could well be an interpolation added later by a follower of Paul. See note by editor Victor P. Furnish, *The Harper Collins Study Bible: New Revised Standard Edition* (London, 1989), 216. A. N. Wilson, *Paul: The Mind of the Apostle* (New York, 1997), 143.

Page 44: *je, tu, nous,* 18.

Page 49: *Paul: The Mind of the Apostle*, 140.

Page 70: Paul calls Phoebe *diakonos,* a masculine noun he applies as well to male colleagues, more deacon than deaconess, which suggests a subordinate capacity. See Mary Getty-Sullivan, *Women in the New Testament* (Collegeville, 2001), 255. The controversy over "Junia" as female (Junia) or male (Junias) continued well into the twentieth century. In the 70's the RSV called her "Junias," presumably because a woman could not possibly have been an apostle. See Eldon Jay Epp, *Junia: the First Woman Apostle* (Minneapolis, 2005).

Page 72: Pliny the Elder, *Natural History: A Selection,* trans. John F. Healy (London, 1991), 138.

Page 76: "World's end came and went, but jokes haven't stopped," *International Herald Tribune,* May 23, 2011.

Page 84: "The Burden of Isis" in *The Burden of Isis: Being the Laments of Isis and Nepthys,* trans. James Teackle Dennis (London, 1910), 37.

Page 86: Nelle Morton, *The Journey Is Home* (Boston, 1988), 41.

Pages 80, 81, 84, 86, 93: I am indebted to Brian Greene for his highly readable account of contemporary notions of physical reality that informed these pages. *The Fabric of the Cosmos: Space, Time, and the Texture of Reality* (New York, 2004).

Page 91: *The Annals of Tacitus,* 15:44, trans. Arthur Murphy, ed. E. H. Blakeney (New York and London, 1907), 487.

About the Author

Becky Gould Gibson, Ph.D. (UNC-Chapel Hill, 1977), taught English and Women's Studies at Guilford College until her retirement in 2008. Her poems have appeared in journals and anthologies, to include *Kalliope*, *Feminist Studies*, *The Comstock Review*, *The Chattahoochee Review*, *Tampa Review*, *Poetry South*, and *The Southern Poetry Anthology: Volume VII* (Texas Review Press, 2014). Gibson has published seven poetry collections, notably, *Aphrodite's Daughter* (2006 X. J. Kennedy Prize, Texas Review Press, 2007); *Need-Fire* (2005 Poetry Book Contest, Bright Hill Press, 2007); and *The Xanthippe Fragments* (St. Andrews University Press, 2016). The last two books give voice to women whose words are missing from the historical record: Hild, Abbess of Whitby (615-680), and Socrates' wife Xanthippe. *Indelible* is a third poetic sequence in that vein. Becky lives with her husband and their canary in Winston-Salem, NC.

Author photo by Bill Gibson

Previous Winners of The Dogfish Head Poetry Prize

2017 Beth Copeland, *Blue Honey*
The Broadkill River Press, Milton, DE

2016 Mary B. Moore, *Flicker*
The Broadkill River Press, Milton, DE

2015 Faith Shearin, *Orpheus, Turning*
The Broadkill River Press, Milton, DE

2014 Lucian Mattison, *Peregrine Nation*
The Broadkill River Press, Milton, DE

2013 Grant Clauser, *Necessary Myths*
The Broadkill River Press, Milton, DE

2012 Tina Raye Dayton, *The Softened Ground*
The Broadkill Press, Milton, DE

2011 Sherry Gage Chappelle, *Salmagundi*
The Broadkill Press, Milton, DE

2010 Amanda Newell, *Fractured Light*
The Broadkill Press, Milton, DE

2009 David P. Kozinski, *Loopholes*
The Broadkill Press, Milton, DE

2008 Linda Blaskey, *Farm*
Bay Oak Publishers, Dover, DE

2007 Anne Agnes Colwell,
Father's Occupation, Mother's Maiden Name
Bay Oak Publishers, Dover, DE

2006 Scott Whitaker, *Field Recordings*
Bay Oak Publishers, Dover, DE

2005 Michael Blaine, *Murmur*
Bay Oak Publishers, Dover, DE

2004 Emily Lloyd, *The Most Daring of Transplants*
Argonne House Press, Washington, DC

2003 James Keegan *Of Fathers and Sons*
Argonne House Press, Washington, DC

Dogfish Head is the first American craft brewery to focus on culinary-inspired beer recipes outside traditional beer styles and it has done so since the day it opened with the motto "off-centered ales for off-centered people." Since 1995, Dogfish has redefined craft beer and the way people think about beer by brewing with unique ingredients.

Today, Dogfish is among the fastest-growing breweries in the country and has won numerous awards throughout the years. Dogfish Head has grown into a 200+ person company with a restaurant/brewery/distillery in Rehoboth Beach, a beer-themed inn on the harbor in Lewes and a production brewery/distillery in Milton, Delaware.

Dogfish Head currently sells beer in 37 states and the District of Columbia, and is proud to sponsor The Dogfish Head Poetry prize, awarded now for sixteen consecutive years!

if a poet is
anybody,
he is somebody
to whom
things made
matter very little
...
somebody
who is
obsessed
by
Making.

- e.e. cummings

Cape Gazette

BEACH PAPER   CapeGazette.com

17585 Nassau Commons Boulevard, Lewes • 302.645.7700

Titles from The Broadkill River Press

Sounding the Atlantic   **Poetry by Martin Galvin**
     ISBN 978-0-9826030-1-7 $14.95

That Deep & Steady Hum   **Poetry by Mary Ann Larkin**
     ISBN 978-0-9826030-2-4 $14.95

Exile at Sarzanna   **Poetry by Laura Brylawski-Miller**
     ISBN 978-0-9826030-5-5 $12.00

The Year of the Dog Throwers   **Poetry by Sid Gold**
     ISBN 978-0-9826030-3-1 $12.00

Domain of the Lower Air   **Fiction by Maryanne Khan**
     (National Book Critics Circle Award Nominee)
     ISBN 978-0-9826030-4-8 $14.95

Speed Enforced by Aircraft   **Poetry by Richard Peabody**
     (NBA Nominee, Pulitzer Prize Nominee)
     ISBN 978-0-9826030-6-2 $15.95

Dutiful Heart   **Poetry by Joy Gaines-Friedler**
     ISBN 978-1-940120-91-1 $16.00

Necessary Myths   **Poetry by Grant Clauser**
     (Dogfish Head Poetry Prize Winner)
     ISBN 978-1-940120-92-8 $14.95

Postcard from Bologna   **Poetry by Howard Gofreed**
     (National Book Critics Circle Award Nominee)
     ISBN 978-1-940-120-90-4 $15.95

Other Titles from The Broadkill River Press

Lemon Light — Poetry by H. A. Maxson
ISBN 978-1-940120-94-2 — $15.95

Peregrine Nation — Poetry by Lucian Mattison
(Dogfish Head Poetry Prize Winner)
ISBN 978-1-940120-85-0 — $15.95

On Gannon Street — Poetry by Mary Ann Larkin
ISBN 978-1-940120-86-7 — $12.00

The Table of the Elements — Poetry by J. T. Whitehead
(National Book Award Nominee)
ISBN 978-1-940120-93-5 — $15.95

Good with Oranges — Poetry by Sid Gold
(National Book Award Nominee)
ISBN 978-1-940120-83-6 — $16.00

Flicker — Poetry by Mary B. Moore
(2016 Dogfish Head Poetry Prize Winner)
ISBN 978-1-940120-75-1 — $16.95

Rock Taught — Poetry by David McAleavey
(National Book Award Nominee)
ISBN 978-1-940120-88-1 — $16.95

Noise — Poetry by W. M. Rivera
ISBN 978-1-940120-70-6 — $16.95

Contents Under Pressure — Fiction by Ellen Prentiss Campbell
(National Book Award Nominee)
(GLCA New Writers Award Nominee)
ISBN 978-1-940120-82-9 — $16.95

The Broadkill Press The Key Poetry Series (Series One)

The Black Narrows — **Poetry by S. Scott Whitaker**
ISBN 978-0-9837789-3-6 $9.95

Ice Solstice — **Poetry by Kelley Jean White**
ISBN 978-0-9837789-4-3 $8.95

Sediment and Other Poems — **Poetry by Gary Hanna**
ISBN 978-0-9837789-5-0 $9.95

Sound Effects — **Poetry by Nina Bennett**
ISBN 978-0-9837789-6-7 $8.95

Taken Away — **Poetry by Carolyn Cecil**
ISBN 978-0-9837789-7-4 $8.95

Where Night Comes From — **Poetry by Shea Garvin**
ISBN 978-0-9837789-8-1 $10.95

(Series Two)

charmed life — **Poetry by Buck Downs**
ISBN # 978-1-940120-96-6 $10.95

The Stories We Tell — **Poetry by Irene Fick**
(Winner 2014 Best Book of Verse, Delaware Press Association)
ISBN # 978-1-940120-98-0 $9.95

Brackish Water — **Poetry by Michael Blaine**
ISBN # 978-1-940120-99-7 $10.95

Love, War and Music — **Poetry by Franetta McMillian**
ISBN # 978-1-940120-89-8 $9.95

Highway 78 — **Poetry by Susanne Bostick Allen**
ISBN 978-1-940120-80-5 $9.95

FLUX Quanta — **Poetry by James Michael Robbins**
ISBN 978-1-940120-81-2 $10.95

The Broadkill Press The Key Poetry Series (Series Three)

Silence, Interrupted   Poetry by Jim Bourey
(Winner 2016 Best Book of Verse, Delaware Press Association)
     ISBN 978-1-940120-87-4 $9.95

Matchstick & Bramble   Poetry by Lucy Simpson
     ISBN 978-1-940120-87-4 $9.95

Gridley Park (forthcoming)   Poetry by Ronald Wilson
     ISBN 978-1-940120-71-3 $10.95

"Purple, Purple" (forthcoming)   Poetry by Ian Walton
     ISBN 978-1-940120-72-0 $12.95

Other Chapbooks from The Broadkill Press

Loopholes   Poetry by David P. Kozinski
(2009 Dogfish Head Poetry Prize Winner)
     ISBN 978-0-9826030-0-0 $7.00

Fractured Light   Poetry by Amanda Newell
(2010 Dogfish Head Poetry Prize Winner)
     ISBN 978-0-9826030-7-9 $7.95

Salmagundi   Poetry by Sherry Gage Chappelle
(2011 Dogfish Head Poetry Prize Winner)
     ISBN 978-0-9826030-9-3 $9.00

The Softened Ground   Poetry by Tina Raye Dayton
(2012 Dogfish Head Poetry Prize Winner)
     ISBN 978-0-9837789-0-5 $9.00

Constructing Fiction   Essays on Craft by Jamie Brown
     ISBN 978-0-9826030-8-6 $6.00

L'Heure bleu   Meta-Fiction by David R. Slavitt
     ISBN 978-0-9837789-1-2 $11.95

The Homestead Poems   Poetry by Gary Hanna
(Honoring the 75th Anniversary of The Rehoboth Art League)
     ISBN 978-0-9837789-2-9 $10.95

Sakura: A Cycle of Haiku   Poetry by Jamie Brown
(Winner 2013 Best Book of Verse, Delaware Press Association)
     ISBN 978-0-9837789-9-8 $10.95